To Lauren + Ben,
A little "Pittsburgh" t[...]
to congratulate you on [...]ment.
Much happiness + love,
Dr. + Mrs. Stotler

12-27-03

D1242235

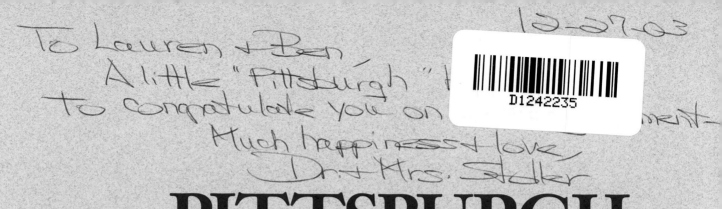

PITTSBURGH

Watercolor Impressions by Robert L. Bowden

Robert Bowden

Published by Hydrangea Books and Sterling Printing
and Graphics, Inc., Pittsburgh, Pennsylvania

ACKNOWLEDGEMENTS

My thanks and appreciation to John Roberts,
co-publisher, for his support on this project
and guidance in the reproduction of my
art, to Tom and Shirley Hamilton for their
coordination and production skills, to
Nancy Hanst for assisting me through
the pitfalls of text and to Jerry Farber for
generously sharing his knowledge and
expertise. A grateful acknowledgement
goes to Diana, my wife, who is a dedicated
collaborator in all of my pursuits.

Copyright 2002 by Robert L. Bowden

All rights reserved. No part of this book may
be used or reproduced in any form whatsoever
without written permission. For information:
Robert L. Bowden, 121 Elysian Street,
Pittsburgh, Pennsylvania 15206;
voice: (412) 363-2081;
fax: (412) 363-6950;
e-mail: wcrob@earthlink.net

ISBN: 0-9707369-2-4

Printed in the United States of America

Cover painting:
SIXTEENTH STREET BRIDGE.
1999, watercolor, 30½″ × 38½″, Artist's collection.

1.

PNC PARK.

2001

watercolor, 18¾″ × 31″

Artist's collection

*The wide space of Smallman Street,
flanked by traditional food
wholesalers and the newer
entertainment venues.*

2.

SMALLMAN STREET IN THE STRIP.

1997
watercolor, 18″ × 23⅜″
Private collection

"Meet me under
Kaufmann's clock."
It's a date all Pittsburghers
have made.

3.
KAUFMANN'S CLOCK.
1995
watercolor, 40″ × 60″
Private collection

KAUFMANN'S

HISTORIC
LANDMARK

Getting close to the river's edge
is not always easy. As I have done
several times in the past, I cross the railroad
tracks and find my way through the
thicket to gain access to a metal-decked
pier. I paint the powerful river from a
place that is safe, but also a little scary.

4.
McKees Rocks Bridge.
2000
watercolor and tempera, 27½″ × 38″
Artist's collection

A long, classy stretch
of Beechwood Boulevard.
Just around the bend is the
starting point of the
annual Pittsburgh 6K race.

5.
BEECHWOOD BOULEVARD BETWEEN
FORBES AND BEACON.
1997
watercolor, 17″ × 23″
Private collection

Two lanes are closed for bridge repair.
It's cold, but sunny. I paint from my car's
front seat. The bridge repair foreman
comes by periodically to watch the painting
develop. He tells me the bridge is a mini-
imitation of the San Francisco Golden
Gate Bridge.

6.
TENTH STREET BRIDGE.
1993
watercolor, 23½″ × 18⁹⁄₁₆″
Private collection

Bernice Moser 1993 Tenth Street Bridge, Pittsburgh

From Phipps Lawn. The Carnegie Museum and Library, The University of Pittsburgh, Phipps Conservatory, Schenley Park — Pittsburgh's original Cultural District.

7.
TOWARDS OAKLAND.
1997
watercolor, 17⅞″ × 23⅛″
Private collection

*Noisy, busy, vital South Side,
once the center of steel production
in Pittsburgh, now a "funky" place.*

8.

CARSON STREET, SOUTH SIDE.

2001

watercolor, 22⅜" × 17¼"

Artist's collection

Heinz Chapel on an extremely hot, humid day. I am painting under the shade of trees and watch one wedding party after another come and go. They have photographs taken, embark in limos and perspire profusely.

9.
HEINZ CHAPEL.
1995
watercolor, 17½″ × 22¾″
Private collection

A*fter two days of painting from an*
"off limits" site, I was packing my gear
to leave, when the guard noticed me.
He told me I wasn't supposed to be there.

10.

SMITHFIELD STREET BRIDGE.

1997
watercolor, 20⅞" × 29⅝"
Private collection

One of the last heavy industrial operations
still billowing. It is partially surrounded
by densely populated neighborhoods.
Soon it will become a redeveloped residential
and commercial site.

11.
HAZELWOOD COKE PLANT.
1994
watercolor, 17¾″ × 23″
Private collection

Robert Bowden 1994

My interest in this building
is the reflections of the surrounding
buildings in its glossy, mirrored
surface.

12.

SAKS FIFTH AVENUE.

1999
watercolor, 21½″ × 29¼″
Artist's collection

A quiet oasis for meeting,
gathering, studying and strolling.

13.
BESIDE CARNEGIE LIBRARY.
1997
watercolor, 18″ × 23″
Private collection

Robert B Bowden April 1997

A Saturday afternoon in this idyllic setting. Except for the dress of the visitors, it could have been one hundred years ago.

14.
CLAYTON CONSERVATORY.
1995
watercolor, 18″ × 23¼″
Private collection

Tomorrow people will be attending mass
at St. Stanislaus. But today is a beautiful warm,
sunny Saturday. Lots of activity on the streets.
Friends show up. "Hi, Claire." "Hi, Jerry." I finish
and have a coffee at Sam's.

15.
TWENTY-FIRST AND SMALLMAN STREETS
IN THE STRIP.
1993
watercolor, 18⅜" × 23¹¹⁄₁₆"
Private collection

Hillside stairways connect neighborhoods
and destinations. This one is from
Troy Hill to Spring Garden, then a short
distance to the Heinz factory.

16.
HEINZ PLANT FROM PROVINCE STREET.
1997
watercolor, 17⅜" × 23⅛"
Private collection

Across Penn Avenue aromas
from the Nabisco plant
drift over the tennis players.
Today, it's Lorna Doones.

17.
MELLON PARK TENNIS.
1992
watercolor, 20″ × 13¾″
Artist's collection

Robert S. Bowden Sept. 1982

The light in late afternoon glitters
on the moving shoppers. The King family's
vitality and exuberance attract me
to paint them in action.

18.
HIGHLAND PARK FARMERS' MARKET.
1993
watercolor, 17″ × 23⅜″
Private collection

A request for an art demonstration
gave me the opportunity once again
to paint this beautifully
proportioned space.

19.
SCULPTURE COURT, CARNEGIE MUSEUM.
2001
watercolor, 24″ × 29″
Private collection

Another hillside view of Pittsburgh,
this one of Arsenal and Lawrenceville.
In another city this site would be
on a bus tour. However, it is
barely accessible by auto.

20.

ABOVE THE FORTIETH STREET BRIDGE.

1999

watercolor and tempera, 30½″ × 38½″

Artist's collection

Our five grandchildren, none of whom live in Pittsburgh, love Kennywood Park. We love to take them there. My boyhood memories of Kennywood return in full force as that old favorite, the Racer, roars by.

21.
RACER.
2002
watercolor, 9″ × 13″
Artist's collection

Complex arches, tall stone entry portals,
sculptures of horses and globes — a beautiful bridge —
and my favorite one to walk. There is a gradual
grade up to a flat span across the river, and
the view of the city, the Strip and the Allegheny
River is spectacular.

22.

Sixteenth Street Bridge
from the North End.

2001

watercolor, 8″ × 14″

Artist's collection

Not hard to get permission to paint
from the inside of this house — it belongs to
our son. A middle-of-winter painting,
very overcast, very cold. The flatness of the Strip
and its industrial look go well with the distant
hillsides of snow and houses on Troy Hill.
A charming bleakness.

23.
FROM HARMAR STREET OVERLOOKING
THE STRIP AND THE ALLEGHENY RIVER.
1993
watercolor, 17⁹⁄₁₆″ × 22⁹⁄₁₆″
Private collection

Parks play a big role in making city living desirable. Within a stone's throw there are a skating rink, tennis courts, a running track and picnic areas. Only a little farther away are a golf course, a conservatory, a nature center and two great universities.

24.

VIEW FROM SCHENLEY PARK.

2000

watercolor, 7″ × 11″

Artist's collection

Robert S Bowden   October, 2000

I knocked at the door of the house where
I chose to set up for this night painting
of the Immaculate Heart of Mary Church,
the dominating structure of Polish Hill.
The homeowners generously agreed to provide
the electric power I needed for a lamp,
my light source. However, they were not
interested in what would materialize.
They never came out to look. So it goes.

25.
NIGHT ON POLISH HILL.
1999
watercolor and tempera, 30½″ × 38½″
Private collection

List of Watercolors

Cover painting: SIXTEENTH STREET BRIDGE. 1999, 30½″ × 38″

1. PNC PARK. 2001, 18¾″ × 31″
2. SMALLMAN STREET IN THE STRIP. 1997, 18″ × 23⅜″
3. KAUFMANN'S CLOCK. 1995, 40″ × 60″
4. McKEES ROCKS BRIDGE. 2000, 27½″ × 38″
5. BEECHWOOD BOULEVARD BETWEEN FORBES AND BEACON. 1997, 17″ × 23″
6. TENTH STREET BRIDGE. 1993, 23½″ × 18⁹⁄₁₆″
7. TOWARDS OAKLAND. 1997, 17⅞″ × 23⅛″
8. CARSON STREET, SOUTH SIDE. 2001, 22⅜″ × 17¼″
9. HEINZ CHAPEL. 1995, 17½″ × 22¾″
10. SMITHFIELD STREET BRIDGE. 1997, 20⅞″ × 29⅝″
11. HAZELWOOD COKE PLANT. 1994, 17¾″ × 23″
12. SAKS FIFTH AVENUE. 1999, 21½″ × 29¼″
13. BESIDE CARNEGIE LIBRARY. 1997, 18″ × 23″
14. CLAYTON CONSERVATORY. 1995, 18″ × 23¼″
15. TWENTY-FIRST AND SMALLMAN STREETS IN THE STRIP. 1993, 18⁹⁄₁₆″ × 23¹¹⁄₁₆″
16. HEINZ PLANT FROM PROVINCE STREET. 1997, 17⅜″ × 23⅛″
17. MELLON PARK TENNIS. 1992, 20″ × 13¾″
18. HIGHLAND PARK FARMERS' MARKET. 1993, 17″ × 23⅜″
19. SCULPTURE COURT, CARNEGIE MUSEUM. 2001, 24″ × 29″
20. ABOVE THE FORTIETH STREET BRIDGE. 1999, 30½″ × 38½″
21. RACER. 2002, 9″ × 13″
22. SIXTEENTH STREET BRIDGE FROM THE NORTH END. 2001, 8″ × 14″
23. FROM HARMAR STREET OVERLOOKING THE STRIP AND THE ALLEGHENY RIVER. 1993, 17⁹⁄₁₆″ × 22⁹⁄₁₆″
24. VIEW FROM SCHENLEY PARK. 2000, 7″ × 11″
25. NIGHT ON POLISH HILL. 1999, 30½″ × 38½″

Back cover painting: ON THE CARNEGIE MELLON CAMPUS. 2002, 7″ × 9″